CW01080753

# CONTENTS

*'Scarborough is incomparable, both as a seaside resort and as a centre for exploring the Yorkshire coast and moors.*

*Well has this delightful place been called the Queen of Watering Places, for it offers something for everyone. Pleasure and beauty are the keynotes, and the place has made the most of it's natural charm.'*

**Yorkshire Revealed,
Geoffrey Douglas Bolton, 1955.**

# Welcome

Welcome to Scarborough and The Central Tramway Company.

The story of The Central Tramway begins in the glorious period of Scarborough's Victorian past when visitors to the seaside town crowded the beaches and promenades. In this brief history of the Tramway we'll discover why and how the founders built the Tramway at such an exciting time of engineering innovation and cultural change. We'll also explain how the funicular operates today.

We're still proud to be continuing the tradition of carrying passengers up and down the cliff from the town to the seafront of the South Bay over 135 years on, and preserving a part of the heritage of the North Yorkshire coast for future generations.

At Central Tramway we also understand that there's nothing better than a great British family day out at the seaside with fish and chips, buckets and spades, and a ride on a donkey. Scarborough has so much to offer all the family, and kids especially love riding on the funicular, which is why at the end of this book you'll find some activities to inspire and entertain your little ones.

Thank you for supporting the Tramway and we hope to see you again soon,

**All the team at**
**Central Tramway Company, Scarborough.**
**Summer 2017**

# FRIENDS OF CENTRAL TRAMWAY

Central Tramway has, since the Victorian times, been an integral part of Scarborough life. Throughout that time new challenges and regulations have meant that the Tramway has had to be maintained to the highest possible standard. There is however a responsibility not only to present day passengers, but also to those who will come in the future. The Town Council, Scarborough and District Civic Society, and the Heritage Railway Association are also such guardians, and we are fortunate to count them as our friends.

As the Mayor of the Borough of Scarborough for 2017/18 and on behalf of the Council, I pay tribute to the Central Tramway Company, Britain's oldest surviving cliff tramway company founded in 1881, which, since it began, has provided a much needed and valued public transport service for our community and for thousands of tourists visiting Scarborough and the Borough annually.

From the tram you are rewarded with stunning views of the beautiful South Bay, South Cliff Gardens and around the coast.
I wish the Central Tramway Company continued success.

**Cllr Martin Smith**
**Mayor of the Borough of Scarborough**

I am delighted to contribute a few words to this informative and attractive brochure on the Central Tramway Company. The term "tramway" is usually associated with street-running trams, and Scarborough once had such a system: the Scarborough Tramways Company, which opened in 1904 and closed in 1931.

How different from the Central Tramway Company, which opened in 1881 and is still at work! As such it is a venerable, but vibrant, and thus valued, member of the Heritage Railway Association, the body concerned with the preservation and advancement of heritage railways and tramways in the British Isles. May the Company long continue to serve Scarborough's inhabitants and visitors!

**Geoffrey Claydon, CB**
**Vice-President, National Tramway Museum**
**Director, Heritage Railway Association**

The Central Tramway Company has the outstanding record of providing a valuable service in Scarborough since 1881. It is a pleasure and a privilege to see what a wonderful job has been made of updating this essential transport link down to the beach and it is now set for many more years of service.

The Civic Society appreciates the care given to restoring and maintaining this delightful part of Scarborough's history and is proud to have the company as a corporate member.

**Adrian Perry**
**Honorary Secretary of the**
**Scarborough and District Civic Society**

# Victorian Scarborough

The Scarborough that we know today, of holidaymakers, entertainment for the family, and seaside fun has its roots in the 1600s. Visitors had been arriving in Scarborough since the middle of the 17th century following the discovery in 1626 by Thomasin Farrer of the acidic water running into the south bay(the bar and restaurant at the Spa is now named in her honour). Scarborough soon emerged as a Spa Town initially attracting wealthy visitors to take the waters and enjoy the fresh sea air. It remained comparatively isolated however, with no canal or major road links to the rest of the UK until the mid 19th century.

As the town grew local amenities improved such as the introduction of steam pumps at Cayton Bay, which saw an increase in the volume of water supplied to the town, as well as an improvement in the sewage system. Other services such as transport links also improved, the construction of the railway line and arrival in 1845 of the first passengers to the newly built railway station brought only a modest increase in numbers.

The iconic Grand Hotel with its prominent position on the South Bay was completed in 1867 to much fanfare both nationally and internationally. Designed by Hull architect Cuthbert Broderick it was lauded as one of the biggest hotels in the world, and one of the first giant purpose built hotels in Europe. The hotel and local attractions initially only attracted the wealthy who could afford to take holiday time away from home, as Derrick Boothroyd wrote in his 1976 book '**Nowt as Queer as Folk**';

> *'In the nineteenth century Scarborough's development as a seaside resort continued apace but the resort concentrated on preserving its selectness and few concessions were made to the tastes of the masses. Evening dress was de rigeur on the Spa after sundown and entertainment was confined to an orchestra and one or two pierrot shows'.*

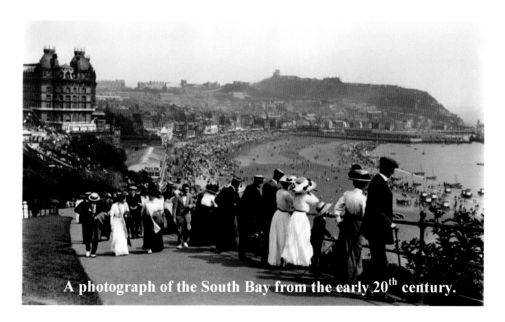

**A photograph of the South Bay from the early 20th century.**

This was to change in 1871 with the introduction of Bank Holidays. The chance of a day out and special fare offers meant that workers from the industrial north could take the opportunity to visit the coast. Visitors sought attractions where they could spend hours rather than the leisurely days or weeks that wealthier tourists had enjoyed. To satisfy this new type of visitor coming to Scarborough, new attractions and amenities soon developed along both the North and South Bays, many of which survive to this day. Foreshore Road was completed in 1871, connecting the North and South Bays. A Pier was built in the North Bay in 1868 despite much local opposition, but was destroyed by gales just 37 years later in 1905. Valley Bridge was opened in 1865 and in 1875 the Spa Tramway connecting the Spa in the South Bay to the hotels and houses above was opened.

It was at this time a new aquarium was built in 1877. The underground aquarium was the predecessor of the current arcades and activities along the Foreshore Road and included penny arcades similar to those on the seafront today. Work began on the Marine Drive in 1896, and was eventually completed with the final section of the road joining the north and south bays in 1902. Between 1887 and 1914 many of Scarborough's famous gardens were also built, thus completing much of the iconic landscape visitors still enjoy today. With the influx of tourists and visitors came an increase in the local population to keep up with the demands of busy hotels and attractions. The population of Scarborough had increased from 13,000 in 1851 to 33,000 in 1891. It was at this time of huge development and social change that the Central Tramway was built next to the opulent Grand Hotel.

View of the Grand Hotel and the Exhibition Hall, which is now occupied by Olympia built by John Woodall Woodall. The Tramway can just be seen between the two buildings.

# HOW THE TRAMWAY BEGAN

The first funicular to be built in the UK was the Spa Tramway in Scarborough in 1875. The second funicular to be built was the Queen's Parade Tramway built in 1878, linking Queen's Parade on the top of the North Bay to the Promenade Pier. However, a cabin broke loose on the opening day and the lift never recovered from that early set back, closing soon after in 1887.

The Central Tramway Company was formed by an enterprising group of local people who between them subscribed for £10,000 worth of shares in the company (approximately equivalent to £1 million today). Among the original shareholders was one Charles Laughton of the Victoria Hotel Scarborough, whose son of the same name went on to become a famous film star.

**An early photograph of the top station, circa 1900.**

The first Chairman of the Company was John Woodall Woodall (1831 – 1905) a Fellow of the Royal Society, four times Mayor of Scarborough, banker, marine environmentalist and general benefactor of Scarborough (see image right). He was passionate about the dangers of over-fishing the North Sea, in the late 19th Century. John Woodall Woodall's family home was the building that is now the Town Hall, which included the St Nicholas Cliff Gardens and a large Exhibition Hall on the site of the current Olympia (see picture on page 11). The Exhibition Hall was designed to hold 5000 spectators and was used to promote the fishing industry.

John Woodall Woodall.

Those early shareholders of the Central Tramway were, in effect, copying the success of the Spa Lift that had been opened six years earlier. The Spa Tramway is now owned by Scarborough Borough Council, having bought out the original limited company, thereby leaving the Central Tramway as the oldest surviving Tramway Company in the UK*. Even to this day it is staggering to think that all the construction and engineering work was done in just six months, between registering the company on the 20th of January and opening to the public on the 1st of August 1881. In 1920 the original coal-powered steam engine that powered the tram was replaced by electric power.

*Source: 'A 1975 centenary: The Scarborough Cliff Lifts' HV Jinks & JH Price

In 1932 Hudswell Clarke & Co of Leeds relaid the track and converted the electricity to AC drive with a 60 horse power motor at the upper station. At the same time, the local coach building company of Plaxton's supplied new carriages. The new cars entered service in a livery of brownish red, the same colours that we have chosen for our refurbishment in 2012.

In 1967 the Purshouse family of Rotherham, took over the majority of the shares in the company. Eric Purshouse (1901 -1991) became Chairman, and his son Lewis (1927 – 2010) became a Director (opposite). Together they had acquired a range of business activities in South Yorkshire. Starting from their butchers business they moved into property development, Rotherham United Football Club, the Regent Theatre in Rotherham, and in 1967 the Central Tramway Company in Scarborough. The Tramway is still in the ownership of the next generation of the Purshouse family today. Eric and his wife Edith used to enjoy holidays at the Grand Hotel in Scarborough. One day they were riding on the Central Tramway and Eric happened to notice that the company was established in the same year as his butchers business. Always open to a new business opportunity, he and Lewis began to acquire a majority shareholding in the company. At this time the Purshouse family formed a good personal and professional relationship with the Temple family of Scarborough. George and Herbert Temple were directors with them through the latter part of the 20th century, and provided the invaluable local knowledge that was to prove essential for the company's continued success.

**Lewis (left) and Eric Purshouse.**

# A New Era

Through the second half of the 20<sup>th</sup> century the Tramway underwent more changes. In 1967 a solid reinforced concrete foundation was laid under the track (still visible today), with the exception of the top 30 yards. In 1975 a fire at the Olympia site damaged the carriages. Two new aluminium carriages were supplied by George Neville Truck Equipment of Kirkby in Ashfield. The future of the Tramway was put in jeopardy in 1976 when pile driving at the Olympia site caused subsidence under the track. The Tramway did not operate for a full year, while repairs were made. The company took the contractors to court and won full compensation for the remedial work and all consequential losses.

A pivotal role in the success of the Company, in more recent years, was played by Chief Engineer, Jim Dungey (1991 – 2012). Jim had worked on the Tramway as a contractor for Brogden and Wilson for many years before deciding to join the Company.

In 2009 the company installed a fully automated drive system, with a new 60 HP electric motor with the objective of enabling a smooth acceleration and deceleration into and out of the stations. This automation took away dependency on manual driving, and consequently improved the safe operation of the facility. In 2016, the Company installed a new hydraulic disc brake, manufactured by Twiflex Ltd.

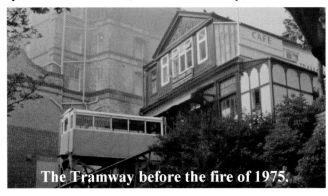

The Tramway before the fire of 1975.

In 2012, the company began a major refurbishment of the stations and carriages, which continues to this day. The inspiration for the refurbishment came from a report by two local architects, Barry and Belinda Denton. They provided an invaluable blue-print of how the Tramway could look. During this busy period of change, the staff at the Tramway became fully engaged in the refurbishment, among them Colin Paxton, with over thirty years of service, Alan Braidley, Maintenance Manager and our Operations Manager, Drew Martin. Jason Beardsley of Sign Experience has helped re-create the Victorian feel of the Tramway with his design and creative skills (www.signexperience.co.uk).

The objective of the refurbishment was to bring back the original features of the Tramway to their former glory. This included a return to the original livery of burgundy and cream. Over the following pages you can see the dramatic difference this has made to the Tramway and its surroundings.

In July 2012, The Mayor of the Borough of Scarborough, Councillor Helen Mallory unveiled a Heritage Blue Plaque (right) to acknowledge the contribution of the Central Tramway to Scarborough's social and industrial heritage. This can now be seen above the entrance to the Parlour Tea Rooms by the top station.

# Refurbishment of 2012

BEFORE

AFTER

BEFORE

AFTER

Bottom photograph courtesy of Roy Hampson

Bottom photograph courtesy of Roy Hampson

BEFORE

AFTER

# HOW THE TRAMWAY WORKS

The Central Tramway is a funicular railway, the principle of which is that two carriages are permanently attached to each other by means of steel hauling ropes, or cables. These cables run in deep grooves over a central pulley, which is driven by a motor.

The Central Tramway has two tracks running between Marine Parade in the centre of Scarborough at the Top Station, and Foreshore Road, on the South Bay Beach at the bottom station. Each track is 234 feet or 79m long, and has an incline of 1 in 2.8.

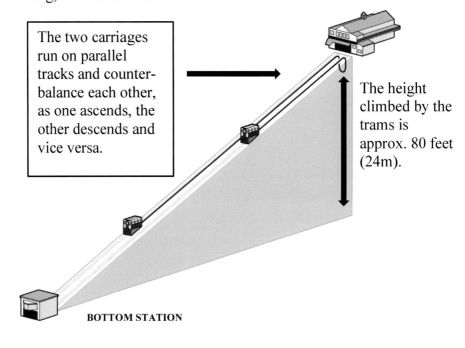

**TOP STATION**

The two carriages run on parallel tracks and counterbalance each other, as one ascends, the other descends and vice versa.

The height climbed by the trams is approx. 80 feet (24m).

**BOTTOM STATION**

Technical illustration by Richard Palmer
(NB. Not to scale) www.richardpalmergraphics.com

The Tramway has an electronically controlled drive system, which picks up signals from the carriages passing over the track. This system was newly installed for the opening of the 2009 season. The new system incorporates important safety features including controlled slowing and stopping of the carriages into the stations.

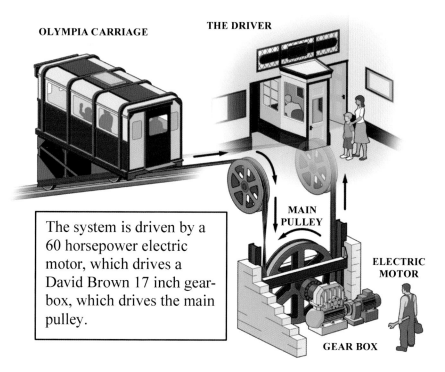

OLYMPIA CARRIAGE

THE DRIVER

The system is driven by a 60 horsepower electric motor, which drives a David Brown 17 inch gear-box, which drives the main pulley.

MAIN PULLEY

ELECTRIC MOTOR

GEAR BOX

The 4 hauling cables, attached to the two carriages, are special high strength, compacted cables, each one 19 mm thick, with a breaking strength of 32 tons. Therefore the four cables are capable of carrying 128 tons. The two carriages, when fully loaded can weigh up to 7.5 tons each, or 15 tons in total, which is well within the capacity of the 128 ton breaking strength.

Technical illustration by Richard Palmer
www.richardpalmergraphics.com

# THE MACHINE ROOM

Alongside the refurbishment of the areas visible to the public (see pages 18-21), the machine room and equipment has also undergone an update. The paintwork of the machinery is now in-keeping with the appearance of the rest of the Tramway. During National Heritage Weekend every year in September you can visit the machine room and see the machinery in action (check our website for details).

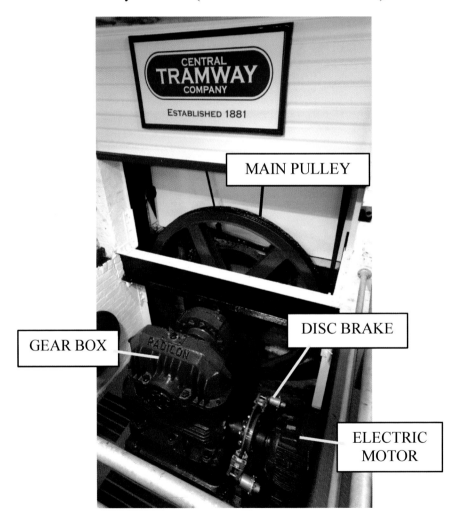

# Schools & the Scarborough Community

The Central Tramway Company is keen to promote school visits where children can enjoy a trip on the Tramway and learn about the rich heritage of Scarborough's Victorian past. Our staff are available to give talks on the history and engineering of the Tramway. We also have educational resources and activity sheets for use in the classroom.

For Early Years Foundations Stage and Key Stage 1 children we have a children's illustrated book all about one little boy's experience of travelling on the Tramway for the first time with his Grandad, which can be used as part of lesson planning around a visit (see page 30).

If you are a teacher who would like to bring your class to the Tram for a fun, educational visit please contact us at info@centraltramway.co.uk.

Similar visits can also be organised for historical and social groups in the area. For example the Tramway has hosted events for the Women's Institute and the Scarborough and District Civic Society where adults too can learn about the Central Tramway and Scarborough's past.

---

## The Tramway on Social Media

You can contact the Central Tramway via our social media pages:

@centraltramway

/centraltramway

@centraltramway

You can also leave a review for us on Trip Advisor. Thank you for sharing your experiences at the Central Tramway.

# FUN FOR THE KIDS

We hope that you and your family have had a great time at the Central Tramway today. Here are some fun activities we hope you will enjoy during and after your visit.

## QUICK QUIZ

1. When was the Tramway built?
2. Who was the first Chairman of the company?
3. Which family took over the majority shares in 1967?
4. What is the cable that moves the trams made from?
5. What is the breaking strength of each cable?
6. How long is the track?
7. How much can each carriage weigh when full?
8. What is the name of the hotel next to the Tramway?

Illustration by Kerry Dunning.
www.kerrydunningillustrations.com

Can you draw a picture of your visit to the Tram? Was the sun shining or did it rain? This is a picture from our children's book Tom and the Tram (see page 30).

## EYE SPY

Can you spot:

Stained glass panel
The Driver
The Rowntrees' advert
Statue of the little boy
The Cupola
5 clocks

## FUN FACT

The cables of the Tramway are so strong they could hold 25 fully grown elephants that each weighed 5 tonnes!!

Illustration by Kerry Dunning.
www.kerrydunningillustrations.com

## MAKE A MODEL TRAM

When you get home try making your own model of a funicular tramway with 2 small cardboard boxes (match-boxes will do) and a piece of string.
Tie the boxes to each end of the string and loop the string over the handle of a door, now pull each end slowly and watch the other end move up and down. Congratulations, you've made your own Tramway, you could even make some figures or models to put in as passengers!
Send us a photo of your model via social media (see page 25).

# SAFETY AT THE CENTRAL TRAMWAY COMPANY

The Health and Safety of our customers and staff is our No1 priority at the Central Tramway Company. The regulatory body responsible for the oversight of funicular railways in the UK is HM Inspector of Mines (HMIM). The HMIM hold meetings twice per annum with all funicular operators as part of their supervisory activities, and pay periodic visits to all the funiculars. The Company has to comply with the Lifting Operations and Lifting Equipment Regulations (LOLER), and as such is inspected every six months. The Company is assisted in its health and safety policy by Coast Risk Management Ltd (www.coastriskmanagement.co.uk). Coast Risk Management help us with risk assessments, emergency drills, first aid training, etc. The Tramway closes for approximately three months every year, from November to the end of January (with the exception of the Christmas period). No stone is left unturned in order to satisfy ourselves that the Tramway is safe for the coming season. In order to ensure that adequate resources are devoted to this task, the company employs its own dedicated and experienced maintenance staff.

# THE FUTURE

The future of the Central Tramway is very closely linked with the future of Scarborough as a tourist destination. As Scarborough grows, with increased domestic tourism and new attractions along the seafront, we look forward to welcoming more visitors to the Tramway to experience the Victorian heritage of the past and how well it serves us in the present. Our primary focus will remain the safe operation of the Tramway, and we look forward to forging closer ties to our friends in the Scarborough and Yorkshire community. Thank you for visiting the Central Tramway and we look forward to welcoming you again soon.

# Available to buy from Central Tramway Company

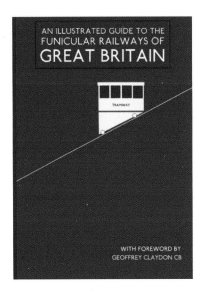

Available to buy at the top station is our guidebook to the **Funicular Railways of Great Britain**.

A comprehensive and informative guide, this 32 page, full-colour paperback offers facts and stats about your favourite heritage tramways around the UK with a handy map to show locations and space to record your visits.

**Tom and the Tram** is a beautifully illustrated children's paperback book for children aged 3-6. It tells the story of one little boy's first ride on the Tram with his Grandad.

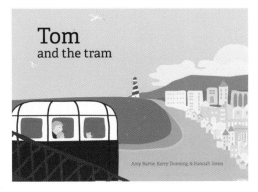

Also available at the top station is an A3 poster of '**How the Tramway Works**', this is a reproduction of the poster that appears under the clock at the top station, as well as a selection of **postcards**, the perfect memento of your trip to the Central Tramway.